LOVE STEENX
By
Chicken Doodle Soup

Meet Napoleon Vaughn Robert Steenx – a guy desperate to love and be loved in blissful monogamy by the woman of his hope-filled dreams, Keener Berensen. Unfortunately, neither she nor any other woman orbiting Steenx's universe, seems interested in beaming down to explore the lonely landscape of his affection-starved heart. Any of you former or current N.A.S.A. (Need A Sweetheart Ally) members feeling the sympathy pains?

And now you're cordially invited to be the fly on the humor-paneled wall, as Steenx engages in hilarious conversation with his best friend and food fanatic, Bank Norwood. Then, after all is said and done amidst the atmosphere of love-scented longing, you may find yourself laughing uncontrollably over the sad fact that sometimes indeed...

BASED ON A CONCEPT BY DONNELL OWENS. IN MEMORY OF HOOBA THE CIRCUS CRAB, WHO DIED TRYING TO SWALLOW HIS OWN SHELL.

LOVE *STEENX*

PRESENTED PROUDLY IN ASSOCIATION WITH ICEBERG TONY'S USED DENTURE DISCOUNTS, SUSHI JERKY NUGGETS AND MOBILE PUBLISHING COMPANY IN A VAN

IT'S WEIRD THAT YAWNING IS CONTAGIOUS, BUT IT'S NOT CONSIDERED A DISEASE. AND THAT CARS NEED BRAKE SHOES BUT NOT SOCKS.

LOVE Steenx

BY
Chicken
DOODLE Soup

iUniverse®

LOVE STEENX

iUniverse books may be ordered through booksellers or by contacting:

iUniverse
1663 Liberty Drive
Bloomington, IN 47403
www.iuniverse.com
1-800-Authors (1-800-288-4677)

ISBN: 978-1-5320-1365-2 (sc)
ISBN: 978-1-5320-1366-9 (e)

Print information available on the last page.

iUniverse rev. date: 02/03/2017

LOVE *STEENX*

by Chicken Doodle Soup

LOVE *STEENX*

by Chicken Doodle Soup

LOVE *STEENX*

by Chicken Doodle Soup

LOVE *STEENX*

by Chicken Doodle Soup

LOVE *STEENX*

by Chicken Doodle Soup

THOUGHTS MR. STEENX SHOULD CONSIDER WHILE WAITING TO BE BLESSED WITH HIS

NAPOLEON DYNA-MATE...

Love only
shows
up
on time...

*...for
   those not
staring at
   their watch.*

LOVE *STEENX*

by Chicken Doodle Soup

LOVE *STEENX*

by Chicken Doodle Soup

If
romance
      isn't
         calling
   your
name...

...perhaps it's because you're using an alias.

LOVE *STEENX*

by Chicken Doodle Soup

LOVE *STEENX*

by Chicken Doodle Soup

The lesson you learn upon discovering yours wasn't a MATCH made in heaven...

*...is
that nobody
smokes
in heaven.*

LOVE *STEENX*

by Chicken Doodle Soup

LOVE *STEENX*

by Chicken Doodle Soup

19

If
you desire someone
on the
partnership roadway
who drives a heart
dirtied with
selfish interests...

...it would
be best to hold
off
until that person
gets a
core wash.

LOVE *STEENX*

by Chicken Doodle Soup

LOVE *STEENX*

by Chicken Doodle Soup

Thankfully,
love
at
first sight...

*...can
sometimes
be
hard
of
hearing.*

LOVE *STEENX*

by Chicken Doodle Soup

LOVE *STEENX*

by Chicken Doodle Soup

Love
makes
the
world
go
round,
but those who
wait
too late...

...foolishly

attempt

to

spin

it

backward.

LOVE *STEENX*

by Chicken Doodle Soup

LOVE *STEENX*

by Chicken Doodle Soup

If you desire to be tightly
fastened
to a love-brew barista,
who will only
serve you a
cup of bitter affection
with no
sugar...

...it's no

doubt

time you

switched to

de-cuff.

LOVE *STEENX*

by Chicken Doodle Soup

LOVE *STEENX*

by Chicken Doodle Soup

Slobbering
over
   someone
with insincere
feelings for
      you...

...only ensures your relationship will be over in a
SPIT
second.

LOVE *STEENX*

by Chicken Doodle Soup

LOVE *STEENX*

by Chicken Doodle Soup

Ripping your
heart
to pieces
because you can't
marry yourself to
the idea of waiting
on
true
love...

*...simply
confirms you're
a
perfect size to
wear
a
shredding
ring.*

LOVE *STEENX*

by Chicken Doodle Soup

LOVE *STEENX*

by Chicken Doodle Soup

The problem
with
the
gift of
love being
free...

...is that so many abusers invalidate it with a discredit card.

LOVE *STEENX*

by Chicken Doodle Soup

46

LOVE *STEENX*

by Chicken Doodle Soup

If you're sad
because
love has
trouble finding
and
kissing your
waiting cheek...

...maybe it's because you're two-faced.

LOVE *STEENX*

by Chicken Doodle Soup

LOVE *STEENX*

by Chicken Doodle Soup

A frightened heart
shrunken by
   disappointment
can easily expand
     to
   try
love again...

*...as
long
as it's
fitted
with
a placemaker.*

LOVE *STEENX*

by Chicken Doodle Soup

AND SO...

Week after week passes as Napoleon leads his life - without hearing even one word from Keener. Having finally moved beyond paralyzing heartbreak and sadness, he has resigned himself to finding true love elsewhere, and is headed out with Bank to pick up their double-dates for the evening, when...

LOVE *STEENX*

by Chicken Doodle Soup

NAPOLEON STEENX WILL RETURN. KINDA LIKE THE WAY
*JAMES BOND ALWAYS RETURNS. BUT UNLIKE ALL THE ACTORS
THAT HAVE PLAYED THE SMOOTH, NOT-SO-SECRET
AGENT, OUR, UH, "HERO" WILL KEEP
SHOWING UP WITH THE SAME
FACE...AND PROBLEM...*

*...ICEBERG TONY WON'T LET HIM FIND A GIRLFRIEND JUST YET,
SO WE CAN KEEP YOU THOROUGHLY ENTERTAINED.
NO NEED TO THANK HIM.*

Check out our quality products at ICEBERG TONY'S USED DENTURE
DISCOUNTS, SUSHI JERKY NUGGETS AND MOBILE PUBLISHING COMPANY
IN A VAN online at *legitandbythebook.com.* Or call us at (818) 288-2901.
Also find us in bookstores both online and...offline??? Yes, you can walk
into a bookstore and find us – this time without fear of a police raid.

FORMER CONVICT ICEBERG TONY THANKS THE FOLLOWING PEOPLE FOR THEIR INSPIRATION IN ASSISTING HIM TO GO STRAIGHT...INTO BOOK PUBLISHING...

*Gerson *"Gerson Electronics"* Coroy

*LaWalrus Bongo – former girlfriend and first female mayor of Sniderpoot, Indiana

*Jonny Quest

*The Five Deadly Venoms

*Breuer Hautenfaust

*GoGo Yabari, Howard Borden, Tiny Tim & the ghost of Re-gifted Christmas Present

*The poor guy in that one movie where his girlfriend broke off their engagement, because he mistook her new hairdo for a canned ham

*Marine Mokensteff – Tony's incredibly sweet neighbor who died completely hopeless, because she failed to convince the lonely women in her sewing circle that heaven will smell like chicken broth and Old Spice

*People who take chances despite the odds

*Oddballs who take people despite the chances (it's called marriage vows)

*People who remind Tony how good God is

*Every family member and friend in his life sentence, uh... *life*. Sorry – it's sometimes hard for Tony to believe he's a free man whose attorney got him released on a miraculous technicality

*Bob

ABOUT US...

Chicken Doodle Soup is a cartoonist who perfected his craft for 27 long years in the exotic temple of the *INTERNATIONAL HOUSE OF PANCAKES* – studying under famed artist, Binky The Wonder Turtle. Mr. The Wonder Turtle is highly acclaimed for his celebrated portraits of 17 U.S. presidents fashioned with unparalleled brilliance, using a special hybrid mixture of semi-gloss paint and Dodger Stadium bacon grease.

Iceberg Tony is an "honest" entrepreneur who prides himself on providing popular commercial products to the general public far below retail-price points. As a generous humanitarian who worries constantly about the less fortunate, he is often heard at charity events delivering his passionate, teary-eyed proclamation that, "Until now, all my parole-board hearings have been rigged."

Donnell Owens is a valued employee at ICEBERG TONY'S USED DENTURE DISCOUNTS, SUSHI JERKY NUGGETS AND MOBILE PUBLISHING COMPANY IN A VAN. Their office, high-demand merchandise and printing press are on wheels for fast getaways, uh, deliveries to customers - and Mr. Owens is to be congratulated for having received a promotion from low-level van wash-and-waxer, to the coveted position of Chief Executive Officer in Charge of Proper Vehicle Tire Pressure.

legitandbythebook.com
(818) 288-2901

Is this business owner and family man
having a bad dream, is he the hideous
result of a science experiment gone
horrifyingly wrong, or is he simply in
dire need of his first cup of morning
coffee? Find out when you meet...

BELVIN SNOIT:
ZOMBIE BALLERINA

COMING SOON FROM
ICEBERG TONY'S USED DENTURE
DISCOUNTS, SUSHI JERKY NUGGETS
AND MOBILE PUBLISHING COMPANY
IN A VAN

legitandbythebook.com
(818) 288-2901

ZOMBIES DON'T TRULY EXIST UNLESS YOUR MOTHER-IN-LAW IS HAVING A HORRIBLY BAD WEEK AND SHE'S YOUR HOUSE GUEST.

Printed in the United States
By Bookmasters